Building Trust Online with your Personal Brand and Social Media

A Short Guide for Car Dealers and their Sales Reps

By Susan Varty and Marc Roginsky
www.headstartsocial.com
© 2014 HeadStart Social Inc.
Drive Digital. Win Customers.

416.746.5335 x 236
www.headstartsocial.com
Drive Digital. Win Customers.

Table of Contents

Building Trust Online with your Personal Brand 1

    What is Personal Branding? 1

    Why Personal Branding? 2

    How do you help others? 3

    Arm Yourself with Research 3

    First, Define Your Passion..4

    Second, Create a Plan..6

    Finally, Put your Plan into Action 7

    The Real Estate Agent Example...8

    More Thoughts on Personal Branding..9

Building Trust Online with Social Media..10

    What is social media?...10

    How does social media build trust? 11

    The Benefits of Social Media 12

    Why should we care about social media?...13

    How is digital marketing different from social media marketing? 14

    About the "Big Four" Social Networks 15

    Twitter...15

    Facebook 16

    LinkedIn 17

    YouTube 17

    What kind of content is appropriate for social media marketing? ...18

    What is not appropriate? 19

    Social Media Do's 19

    Social Media Don't's...19

    Tips for Social Media Selling..20

Tips on How to Get Started in Social Media 20

What resources do I need for effective social media marketing?......21

More About Community Management...22

About Social Media Optimization 23

What should I be tracking and collecting? 23

How does social media help lead generation?..................................24

Get in Touch with HeadStart Social 26

Building Trust Online with your Personal Brand

What is Personal Branding?

- What comes to mind when you hear "Mercedes-Benz", "Honda" or "Ford"? People associate different brands with specific attributes and feelings.

- Personal Branding is similar to product branding – it is used to create positive, memorable associations about you and how you help others.

- Personal Branding is all about building trust and positioning your expertise.

- Expertise contributes to the trust factor.

- Trust generates leads and creates sales opportunities.

- It creates awareness to stay "top of mind" when someone is ready to buy.

- Don't confuse your personal brand with a manufacturer brand – you need to distinguish yourself and the value you bring to the table.

- Your Personal Brand is your passion that you take to market – how do you stand out as a sales specialist and a person? You want to strive to be someone customers can relate to at different levels.

Why Personal Branding?

- The smart way you dress, the polished look of the cars in the showroom, the way your dealership looks – all inspire trust and confidence. But potential customers will only see this if they walk in the door.

- Today most people go online first- how do you get them to walk through the doors of your dealership?

- Position yourself as an expert and a trustworthy person so that people turn to you before they purchase a car.

- You can showcase information you endorse or want to promote. This builds trust and "thought-leadership" in your industry.

- Help others learn about you and to explain specifically how you help them when they are considering a car purchase.

- Potential customers will see you as an involved member of the community, digitally-savvy, on-trend and trustworthy.

- Your personal brand helps you use different marketing techniques than your competition, stand out from the crowd and cut through the noise.

- The prospects will remember you and reach out to you for advice. Congratulations – you just generated yourself a lead!

How do you help others?

- A large purchase like a vehicle means that your potential customers have armed themselves with information. So if you can't be informative, how do you build trust and rapport?

- Personal Branding helps people remember how you can help them.

- Define how you help customers and you will become known for it. For example:

    - "I get my customers the best deals and always beat my competitors' pricing. My customers trust me and always return for another purchase."

    - "I work hard to save my customers' time. They rarely spend an entire afternoon at the dealership to close a sale."

    - "My customers can reach out to me by text and through Twitter. They know I'm the "digital rep" so they can ask me quick questions online while they shop."

    - "I help my potential customers by taking a video of their car if it's a used car or a new model in our showroom. When I respond with video, they are impressed."

Arm Yourself with Research

- If you are using the same techniques as everyone else to meet potential customers, you won't stand out from the crowd.

- Use slogans and calls to action (CTA) such as "Get More Info" and other marketing techniques you can work into your sales calls or materials.

- Read your junk mail. This will give you ideas on how to get someone's attention (or not). How compelling are the offers? Which ones would you hang on to?

- Ask people what they read, what websites they like and what events they attend – be sure to advertise there – go to where your customers are.

First, Define Your Passion

- The first step in positioning your brand is to identify what you are all about under the following four categories:

  1. Your Career Success Milestones and Awards

  2. Personal Hobbies and Interests - people love hearing about these!)

  3. Philosophy on Life - what makes you get up in the morning?

  4. Community Events or Speaking Engagements

- Career Success Milestones and Awards include:
  - If you have worked for any big/well known dealerships in the past.
  - The number of years you have you worked at your current dealership.
  - How many years in the industry, performance awards.
  - Relationship building, sales targets, team leadership

- Personal Hobbies and Interests examples include:
    - Hiking, Biking, Chess, Yoga, Science Fiction Novels, TV series (i.e. Game of Thrones, etc.)
    - Most favourite food, vacation spot, sports team
    - Hobbies
    - Family

- Your Philosophy on Life examples include:
    - Why do you enjoy working at the current dealership?
    - What are your customers saying about you?
    - Why do you get return business?
    - "My family is everything to me"
    - "I am obsessed with customer service"

- Community Events or Speaking Engagements include:
    - Community Events, Automotive Conferences, Charity Fundraisers
    - Association Memberships, Board of Trade Meetings, Local Businesses Association

Second, Create a Plan

1. Write down a long-term vision about your career or business – not just about having the latest skill-set or service/product. For example:

   - Go from 100 car sales per year to 150, to 250 car sales per year.

   - Become a sales manager leading a team of representatives.

   - Learn about Fixed Operations to eventually run a service department.

2. Showcase your best recommendations online.
   For example:

   - "Frank helped me find the car I needed – with extras included. He got the deal done fast so that my family and I could still enjoy our Saturday afternoon."

   - Or ask someone to introduce you to someone else or provide a recommendation – what do they say? Is it what you want?

3. Identify the "pain points" you solve for others.
   For example:

   - "I try and understand as much as possible about my customer's family situation to help them make a purchase decision."

   - "We have a lowest price policy that we always deliver on."

   - "I use video to help my clients see what they are getting – and to learn about me."

   - "I help my dealership respond to leads quickly to increase appointment booking rates."

4. Create your unique value proposition (UVP) and define your pitch plus your advertisement.

    Your pitch is your ad – what would you say if you had to put your picture with an ad on a bus?
    For example:

    - "Our customers drive our business. I've been here to serve you for 10 successful years. Call me, email, text me or Facebook me if you need more info about any of our cars!"

    - "We are a family-owned dealership and we understand family needs when it comes to buying cars. Bring your kids with you anytime and we'll keep them occupied while you check out our cars."

    - "I will get you the best deal on our top-selling model – no pressure or surprise fees – guarantee!"

    - "Want to test-drive a car without coming in to our dealership? Check out our dealer YouTube channel for all of my car walk-around videos. You'll know what you are getting yourself into!"

Finally, Put your Plan into Action

- Develop a list of channels where you can showcase and advertise your message/pitch. Use social media networks, blogging, community events, volunteering, speaking engagements, workshops, etc.
  For example:

    - Video blog about cars on YouTube

    - Put your car walk-around videos on YouTube

    - Advertise on Google, Facebook and LinkedIn

- Learn how to meet new potential clients on Twitter
- Join various online car enthusiast groups
- Write your bio for the staff website
- Create a personalized web page/landing page and put it up on your dealership's website.
- Create or complete your LinkedIn profile
- Speak and volunteer at dealership community events

The Real Estate Agent Example

- Real Estate Agents know that personal branding is key to promoting themselves and staying memorable in a competitive market.

- Most car ads have cars – real estate professionals advertise their faces because their product is them. The more you can promote yourself and why people should turn to you, the more likely people will reach out when they have a large purchase to make.

- Most people want and appreciate guidance from someone they trust.

- Referrals gain more traction when you can become an advisor and trusted partner in the second largest purchase a person can make (after buying a home/condominium).

- The more you can promote yourself online and offline, the more "top of mind" you'll be when people start considering a new or used vehicle.

- More experienced car sales representatives have built their network over years and years – personal branding and self-promotion can help you catch up quickly.

More Thoughts on Personal Branding

- "It's all about your customers" – focus your strategy around your customers and their needs.

- Authenticity – be true to yourself. Otherwise, you will lose credibility.

- Celebrate successes – doesn't have to be "showing off", just showing confidence.

- Leverage all of your projects/passions as a springboard for building your social networks online and offline.

- Be bold, try something new – something that your colleagues are reluctant to try – embrace new technologies and channels of communication with your prospects and clients.

Building Trust Online with Social Media

What is social media?

- Social media can be defined as an online community between two or more people discussing topics that interest them.

- People use social networks to share all kinds of information, including cars they are thinking about purchasing.

- Some social networks are "open" like Twitter – where you can talk to anyone. Other social networks require membership and have more privacy settings.

- Increasingly, more and more businesses are using social media to communicate with potential customers online by building "conversation" communities around a product or service.

- Social media has become a part of many peoples' daily routines, which makes it a perfect platform for digital and word-of-mouth marketing online.

- Businesses use social media marketing channels to strike up conversations with consumers or anyone in their target market. They can also ask for customer feedback and run new marketing campaigns.

- Many businesses have customer service representatives monitoring social media channels constantly so that they can address any questions and requests.

- Individuals/car buyers are not only consumers of information - they refer and often influence others when they make purchasing decisions.

- Just as it was with the development of Internet and websites - social media is not a passing fad, and it is not going to go away. In fact, the opposite has occurred, its use and acceptance is continuing to grow with a dramatic increase in the number of users from all walks of life and age categories.

How does social media build trust?

- Social media acts as the public storefront to inspire visits to your website. It can make or break your reputation with your potential customer.

- People typically don't know your website address. They do Google searches, look up your page on Facebook or Twitter. They may not see your website or ads at all except what their friends share on social networks.

- When people ask for referrals – it's based on trust – they know their friend will refer them a great salesperson, product or service.

- Google reviews and Facebook reviews, testimonials, and other rating sites tell others online what to expect when they visit. This is a key component of building trust.

- Great reviews by strangers and recommendations from friends are very reassuring. It often makes the difference when they decide to visit you or your competition.

- Good content on your Facebook page (and other networks) shows that you are involved in the community, having fun and providing useful information. This is how you communicate online that you are a great dealership to visit.

- It's important to maximize the free, public channels available to your dealership. Great content and a robust presence on social media channels help to build trust.

The Benefits of Social Media

- It has the ability to amplify your marketing messages and reach potentially massive audiences (at extremely low costs in comparison with traditional advertising and marketing).

- You can maintain and keep-up-to-date with a community of customers and potential customers through social media channels, which is often cheaper than direct mail or email newsletters.

- By using social media, dealerships can reach their customers when the timing is critical for purchasing a vehicle.

- Better yet, potential customers reach out to you because they are part of your dealership social network community and feel "in the loop" about the latest deal or offer.

- You can build online relationships that position yourself as an expert in what you do. This builds trust and you become the "go-to" person when they are ready to purchase a product or service.

Why should we care about social media?

- Google reviews and now Facebook reviews (and other third-party online review sites) can impact your business reputation when people are deciding what dealership they should go and visit.

- Social media use is increasing rapidly, and the mobile smartphone and tablet market is helping to assist easy access to online communications. Mobile devices allow social media access 24/7, including mainstream news and information.

- Many younger people are not as committed to one brand of vehicle and go to friends and strangers on social networks to see what's "on trend" or what everyone else is purchasing.

- Just like your dealership staff get referrals, referrals through word-of-mouth is being transferred into an online world.

- Conversations that used to be offline and limited in number - if you didn't interact with many others - are now taking place with hundreds, if not thousands of friends and followers online.

- Good content that is shared, helps your SEO (improves your ranking with Google).

- How a Honda dealership used cookie recipes to drive sales: http://www.drivingsales.com/blogs/DrivingRetention/2011/11/29/how-did-howdy-honda-drive-customers-to-their-facebook-page-with-cookie-recipes

How is digital marketing different from social media marketing?

- When people say digital marketing, they are usually referring to digital advertising - a one way announcement using digital ads such as banner images or Facebook advertising, etc.

- Unlike a lot of digital advertising, social media marketing is based on conversations with 2 or more people with similar interests who form part of an online community.

- People use social networks to share all kinds of information, including cars they are thinking about purchasing.

- The introduction of the smartphone means that everyone has access to their friends and family through social networks – amplifying traditional "word of mouth" referrals and information sharing.

- In general, the following components can be included in digital marketing:
    - Having a strong website presence and generating traffic through word-of-mouth, or online contests and campaigns.

    - Purchasing online advertising (such as Google AdWords or web advertising such as banner ads).

    - Permission-based email marketing to a list of customers or potential customers.

    - Search Engine Optimization (SEO).

    - Social media – because it's online – it's often included under the category of digital marketing.

About the "Big Four" Social Networks

- Facebook, Twitter, LinkedIn, YouTube are commonly referred to as the "big four" social media networks.

- Facebook is usually for personal use but advertising can be very effective based on the data they have about consumers at their fingertips. Many companies use Facebook as their online marketing platform to reach car shoppers.

- Twitter is the real-time, "young" network where people tweet about topics that interest them.

- LinkedIn is a business-focused network where people have a work-related profile and are open to business opportunities.

- YouTube allows people to post and share videos.

- Other networks include Google+, Pinterest, and Quora – find out where your prospects hang out and go there!

- Now, with the advent of mobile-based technologies, social media has become even more accessible by more people, of various ages, professions and social classes (demographics).

- More people can access social media platforms (smart phones, tablets, laptops) on the go at any time of the day.

Twitter

- Twitter is a text-based network where people make "announcements", known as tweets, to share links, up-to-the-minute information or just what they are doing in general.

- Companies can monitor Twitter for specific key word phrases to determine if there is interest in products or services.

- There is no need for anyone to be "friends" or be "connected" on Twitter.

- Introductions and conversations can occur (publicly) as long as you have someone's user name.

- A custom Twitter background page for the account is recommended so that visitors have your contact information.

- Promoted tweets (digital ads) based on keywords can be purchased.

Facebook

- Facebook users spend quite a long time on the site versus a traditional website.

- But more importantly, information about marital status, hometown, what people LIKE, sex, age and other targeted information provides an attractive opportunity for advertising.

- Many people LIKE brands on Facebook for contests, deals and customer service questions.

- The ads experiencing the most success are targeted specifically by location, demographic and reach people when the timing is right.

- "The average amount of time users spend on Facebook is miles ahead of Twitter. The typical session on Facebook is 23 minutes and 21 seconds; on Twitter, it's 13.1 minutes." http://www.fastcompany.com/1721054/americans-spend-twice-as-much-time-on-facebook-than-twitter

LinkedIn

- LinkedIn is one of the oldest social networks (2003) that allows its users to create a profile and a company profile for business networking.

- Company pages showcase company-related expertise and also list their employees who have LinkedIn profiles (which helps to demonstrate that you participate online).

- Groups allow you to showcase your individual expertise and to participate in discussions with other individuals who share the same interests as you.

- LinkedIn has the largest "mature" demographic that has a more spending power than the younger generations on Facebook and Twitter.

- Ads purchased for this network can also be targeted to a specific audience, including employer name and local community.

YouTube

- Video is uploaded non-stop onto YouTube every day (48 hours of content every minute).

- Having a video blog (vlog) can be a way to showcase your dealership and the cars you'd like to sell.

- A good example would be recording and posting a video with car-related content, for example comparing various models of vehicles (coordinate with your corporate marketing department as to what car topics you can share publicly on YouTube).

- If one person hosts the video, it can bring a face to the name at your dealership. People might come by to speak with the host or whoever who may be profiled in the video.

- Videos increase trust because viewers have already seen the dealership and get to know the people who work there to ask for them by name.

- Videos make it easier for people to walk-in, refer or share content with others.

- Good lighting and sound is important - as well as being consistent and uploading content at regular times if vlogging is going to be part of your digital strategy.

- Having a video presence is really good for Search Engine Optimization in general, especially if the content is transcribed into text (so it can be indexed by Google more easily).

What kind of content is appropriate for social media marketing?

- Auto industry articles, news, events and traditional online media content can be shared easily through social networks and showcase your expertise. There are many auto-related news and online tools that appeal to car buyers.

- Employee profiles and videos. People get to know the staff and know exactly who to talk to if they would like to visit.

- Stories that the dealership wants to write about on their blog and share online. Usually these are stories about people and what's different about their vehicles, day-in-the-life of the dealership, industry events, etc.

- Dealership generated contests and offers such as daily and weekly deals, specials and incentives. Usually anything that can be done in print can be done online and shared through social networks.

What is not appropriate?

- Anything that reveals detailed customer information to the public without their permission or knowledge.

- Content or statements about politics, sex or religion.

- Content or statements that are inflammatory or insulting, such as a personal attack on an individual or company.

- If you are not sure the content is appropriate, don't put it online.

Social Media Do's

- Do connect with others and talk about industry-related topics.

- Do listen and get to know others before joining online conversations.

- Do take the time to write a polished and professional message or update.

- Do keep an open mind about integrating social media into your daily marketing activities.

Social Media Don't's

- Don't write about how they can purchase a vehicle as your first online conversation.

- Don't rush to put anything online. This results in poor content, spelling and grammatical errors that reflect negatively on your brand.

- Don't force anyone to join networks—or add people to a community who don't give their permission.

- Don't try to sell immediately after connecting on any social network. People use social networks when they are relaxed and want to interact with friends and family first.

Tips for Social Media Selling

- Social media sales can be direct to consumer only after a relationship is established and they have been "engaged" in a conversation online.

- Social media sales are not usually direct from individual to individual (like a cold call).

- It takes time to build the trust required to generate a sale and it is important to ensure the timing is right based on someone's status updates and interests.

- Conversation around common interests and responding in a timely manner builds trust. Build trust first, then sell politely.

- If you are too aggressive in your conversations and they are geared to sell, not create curiosity about what you do, people may block your connection, hide your updates and most likely will go elsewhere. Showcase your expertise in a professional way.

Tips on How to Get Started in Social Media

- Social media networks will drive traffic to your website so it's important to review your own website presence and make sure it is up-to-date.

- A blog is highly recommended to have something to share on social media networks. Instead of driving traffic to another news website, you can drive traffic to your own.

- Communicate your social media ideas and initiatives with all of your staff.

- Get training for your entire staff on how to create appealing content.

- Assign or hire a full-time Community Manager with good customer relationship and communication skills.

- Build one community at a time on each platform.

- Integrate messages and learn the (free) tools, such as TweetDeck and HootSuite to share on all networks.

- Track statistics and metrics at specific time intervals.

- Create a social media communications policy based on your customer service policy and privacy policy.

- Ensure that your staff does not create company-specific social media sites or online properties without dealership management approval.

What resources do I need for effective social media marketing?

- Participation in social media by every employee at the dealership (on an individual level) WILL result in increased promotion online and more sales.

- However, success often depends on having one person in charge of social media on a day-to-day basis called a Community Manager.

- A Community Manager is a communications and social media enthusiast with excellent interpersonal skills.

- A Community Manager is constantly and consistently monitoring and "engaging" people in online conversations and creating content that is relevant to the dealership audience.

- Potential customers often get to know the Community Manager first because they are "front-line" staff. Leads are often passed along to Sales Representatives.

- High quality content, a large community, and consistent dealership community management leads to more word-of-mouth referrals, and the more indirect leads and sales.

More About Community Management

- Community Management is a new role usually performed by an IT support person or someone who is social network or website/internet savvy.

- They work closely with your Digital Marketing/Advertising team to ensure that dealership-generated content is available to everyone online.

- A Dealership Community Manager is highly recommended, as he/she will keep on top of competitive intelligence, respond immediately when people reach out to them online and push out interesting content to their dealership community of potential customers.

- A Dealership Community Manager will also be your "customer relationship manager" engaging, communicating and responding to the community of the consumers and making sure that all of them have a positive experience when interacting with your dealership/ organization.

- Good customer support and a quick response coupled with a positive overall experience WILL have a positive impact on the future referrals and sales.

- The Community Manager may also become your lead appointment setter if they are fully integrated into the sales cycles at your dealership.

About Social Media Optimization

- Car shoppers now expect (more than ever) that companies have a social media presence.

- Many write reviews on Google and Facebook about their experiences at a dealership. This has a big impact on others and whether or not they decide to visit your dealership.

- After paid results, "organic" results often show dealerships who are the most active on any of the Big Four networks.

- Google tends to rank the most up-to-date content first, including publicly available information on social networks, such as Twitter.

- When people comparison shop, they are primed and ready to buy - that's when they search - and that's when you want to be at the top of the list. Use every channel to keep you top of mind with your potential customers.

What should I be tracking and collecting?

- Information about the type of prospect that comes in to see you in person versus the type of prospect who interacts with you online first.

- Permission-based email addresses through social media posts, draws, offers, Facebook applications, contests and ads.

- Basic number codes can be used on social media posts, coupons and digital ads so you can tell where people are coming from. Hidden websites or landing pages can also be used so you can see how effective your campaigns are from specific social networks or digital advertising.

- More advanced tracking can be set up and viewed in Google Analytics. Most social networks provide basic analytics.

- How many people visit the website after visiting a social network or looking at an ad posted within a social network.

- How many times people are sharing dealership-generated content and what they are "engaged" with the most.

- Lead to sales data to evaluate your campaigns and close ratios so you can take action or move more budget money into something that is successful.

How does social media help lead generation?

- Social media builds trust with your potential customers after seeing your digital ads within the social network itself or on Google.

- Leads and customer questions can be posted directly to Facebook and Twitter. Younger generations look to these channels instead of the Yellow Pages or print advertising.

- People are constantly reaching out to friends and family on social networks, comparing deals and dealerships, incentives, specials and prices online.

- Your content can be shared by a loyal customer and then you are endorsed by their friends and family as a trustworthy place to visit.

- Lead generation is a combination of specific offline and online elements (not just hits to your website.)

- Social media will help you build a free local community over time that will spread your offers and reduce your ad spend.

Notes

Get in Touch with HeadStart Social

- We help car dealers boost their online presence and build trust with their potential customers. Whether it's digital advertising, video car walk-arounds, or an online referral kit for individual reps, we can help at reasonable rates and create a custom solution for you.

- Or let us do the work for you and manage a dedicated marketing person at your dealership. Use our payroll and know-how so you can stay focused on sales and operations.

- We pride ourselves on generating qualified leads in your trading area – and tracking everything - so you know that you are getting the most value for your money.

- www.headstartsocial.com 416.746.5335 x 236

- HeadStart Social helps clients maximize digital channels to generate more leads from a targeted audience. Our core services include Automotive Digital Marketing, Online Personal Branding, Search Engine Marketing (SEM), and Content Marketing.

About the Authors

Susan Varty, Co-founder, has been providing results-oriented communications, digital strategy and marketing advice to corporate clients and businesses since 2006. She is a social media and personal branding educator, copywriter, and non-traditional marketer with technical expertise. Susan is also a guest writer for The Globe and Mail and The Huffington Post.

Marc Roginsky, Co-founder, specializes in an employee-centric and integrated approach to digital and social media marketing to give companies a competitive advantage. Marc's integrated approach allows clients to capture more business development opportunities and convert them to sales as a result. His experience of more than 12 years in the recruiting industry has given Marc a unique perspective on company branding, and how its employees can stand out from the crowd to generate more sales.